Rosemarkie People and Places

A collection of photographs and memories
compiled and edited by

Freda Bassindale

Bassman Books

Published by Bassman Books, Burnside Cottage, Newhall, Balblair, Dingwall, IV7 8LT

First published in 2013

A catalogue record for this book is available from the British Library

ISBN 978-0-9567908-4-2

Printed by Big Sky, The Press Building, 305 The Park, Findhorn, Forres, IV36 3TE

*Dedicated to
Mary MacKenzie
and Pearl Sinclair
who provided
information and
material for use in this
book. Both passed
away earlier this year.*

Introduction

When I first mentioned that I would like to publish a book of Rosemarkie photographs, I got a very enthusiastic reaction. I soon amassed a large number of photos and postcards and I discovered that attached to each photo and postcard was an interesting story.

Apart from a few photos from the Groam House Museum collection, the photos and postcards in this book are from the private collections of a few old Rosemarkie families. The legends attached to the photos and postcards are recollections of events within living memory, or are stories that have been passed down through the families by word of mouth. Memories can be deceptive however, and sometimes no two people will remember the same event in the same way. With this in mind, I make no apology for any historical inaccuracies!

With so many interesting pictures at my disposal, my priority was to choose material that would interest the residents of Rosemarkie and all those who are still in contact with the village, or who are interested in their Rosemarkie roots. I also wanted to record what life was like living in Rosemarkie in the 19th and early 20th century. Information is being lost with each generation that dies out, and even now, it is difficult to put names to faces in some of the older school photos.

I hope you enjoy browsing through this book and that the contents bring back many happy memories.

● Sometime during the 1960s Fortrose Academy pupils were responsible for preparing a project on local history. I was lucky enough to be given access to the written project by the daughter of Tom Lloyd. This included information on Rosemarkie School as recalled by Mrs Sinclair who lived in the Old School when it was converted into a dwelling house. John MacArthur provided me with a copy of an audio project compiled by some Rosemarkie pupils and comprised of interviews with Rod Anderson, Jock Miller, Margaret Crawford and Charlie MacKenzie, on subjects covering forestry,

General Merchant & Refreshment Caterer

milling, schools and Rosemarkie in general. Although I haven't used all of the material in this book, there are some interesting pieces of information which can be used later.

Snippets of information have also been gleaned from the following publications: Random Notes on Old Rosemarkie by Alistair S Fraser JP, Fortrose: A Garden City by the Sea by Dorothy Fraser, The Black Isle: A Portrait of the Past by Elizabeth Sutherland, Highland Doorstep by Kenneth A MacRae, Rosemarkie: A Village History by Rosemarkie WRI. ● I could not have compiled this book without the help of the Rosemarkie people and I have listed the main contributors below. Several others came to me with photos and although I haven't been able to use them all in this book, they have been squirrelled away for another edition sometime in the future.

My grateful thanks are due to the following, who have scoured their lofts for material and who have endured my endless questions over the past few months. Without them, this book would never have happened.

Jenny Paterson; Mary MacKenzie; Marie MacKenzie; Rita Cumming; Isobel Grigor; Elspeth Munro, Muir of Ord; Michael More, Inverness; Helen Duncan; Betty Forrester; Kathleen and Hugh MacKay, Dingwall; Sarella Gallie; Norma Sinclair; Mamie MacIver; Ian and Sheena Basham; Hugh and Greta MacKenzie; Sheila Paterson; Billy Winton; Hilary Aitcheson; Tom and Dorothy Lloyd; Glad MacIver; Billy Hossack; Val MacLean, Inverness; Ann Phillips; Sue Wompra and Alastair Morton of Groam House Museum; Patty MacMillan; Alastair Hossack; Lorna Haines; Kenneth Sinclair, Kessock; Pearl Sinclair; Ann Robb; Susan Seright; Norman Newton; Jenny Parkerson, National Libraries of Scotland; Michael MacDonald, Fortrose and Rosemarkie Golf Club; Dorothy MacDonald; Joanie Mair; Betty MacKenzie; Mary Ross, Fortrose; Jean MacArthur; John MacArthur; Amanda MacKay; Ewenie Clark, Avoch.

And finally, my thanks to Ian Basham for his proof–reading skills and Russell Turner of Bassman Books who has been advising and guiding me throughout this project. He has been responsible for transforming some of the old, faded and sometimes tatty pictures into the very acceptable specimens you now see in this book.

If I have forgotten anyone, sorry!

Freda Bassindale, 2013

Contents

Buildings

An early photo of Kincurdie House, c1896, before the trees hid it from view. Kincurdie Estate was part of a large area of the Black Isle owned by the Rosehaugh Estate. Between the wars the house was leased to the Blackwood family and after World War II was occupied by General Sir Richard O'Connor. It was sold to a consortium headed by Sandy Smith from Avoch in the 1960s and later to a property developer. The house is now divided into flats and the outbuildings converted to homes. Several new houses have been built in the grounds.

Above: This photo is of my mother, Chrissie Winton, who was cook at Kincurdie between the wars. She is on the left, and next to her is the butler, John Hossack from Avoch, known as "John the Butler." Next to him is Margaret MacLennan who was housekeeper and the lady at the front is Mary Munro, the housemaid.

Top right: This group was photographed in the grounds of Kincurdie House some-time in the 40s or 50s when Kincurdie opened its gardens to members of the public with the proceeds donated to The Red Cross. The lady in the white coat is Bernice Smith (Junor) mother of David Smith and Marion Clelland.

Bottom right: Daniel Fraser and Jack Stewart, two shop-owners from Rosemarkie and Fortrose, set up their table at the foot of the path leading from Kincurdie Drive up to the Big House, for the purpose of collecting the entrance money from those attending the open day.

Fairy Glen House, pictured c1910. is situated in the Fairy Glen at the west end of the village. I don't know when it was built, but in 1936, Mr John Paterson bought the house and surrounds, plus Arabella Croft for the princely sum of £1,026.

In the late 1700s, there were several weavers in Rosemarkie and many of the householders grew flax on the land attached to their cottages. The flax was harvested and steeped in the ponds or pows, three of which stood at the front of Fairy Glen House. The pows were filled with water diverted from the Rosemarkie burn via a system of lades and spoots, and in the photograph, taken in 1934, the lighter area at the centre left of the photograph, could be the remains of one of the pows.

The weaving industry in Rosemarkie came to an end in about 1830 due to the heavy taxes imposed on the linen merchants. Wool was the up and coming industry and the large landowners and wool merchants had to be appeased.

There are still some pieces of Rosemarkie linen in the village and I am the proud possessor of a small tablecloth. My ancestors were called Clark and several generations of them were weavers. I like to think that I might own a piece of material made by the hands of my six-times great-grandfather, Thomas Clark.

The pows were also used in the salmon-fishing industry. In winter, when the water froze, the ice was cut into chunks and carted to three local icehouses in Kincurdie Drive, Chanonry Point and the not-so-well-known one underneath Jubilee Cottage on Marine Terrace, to be stored for use by the salmon fishers during the salmon fishing season. The work was cold, but was alleviated by the bottles of whisky supplied to the work party. Apparently, as the day wore on the men became more and more intoxicated and were a source of great amusement for onlookers. According to Rod Anderson

This view of Fairy Glen House was taken in 1934 and shows what could be a pond in front of the house.

in a recorded interview he gave to Mr Donald (Tufty) MacLeod, a teacher in Fortrose Academy who later became its headmaster, the salmon fishers cut the ice and they employed several men with their horses and carts from surrounding farms to transport the ice to the ice-houses. My father once told me that in the 1920s, when he was growing up in the village, he and his friends were also employed to barrow the ice chunks to the ice-houses.

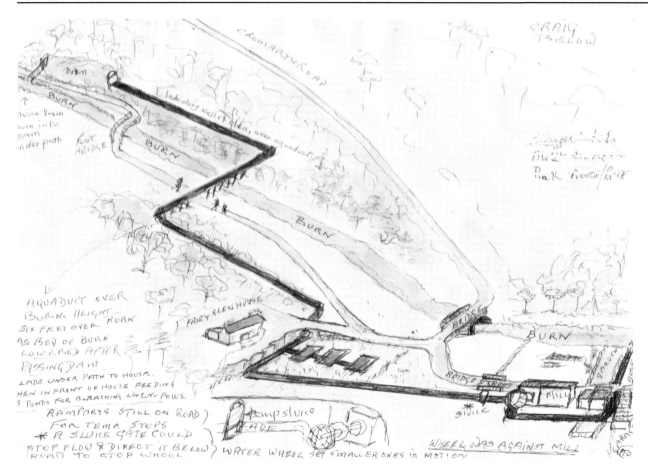

This is a drawing by Betty Forrester, of the system of lades and spoots built to extract the water from the Rosemarkie burn for use in the pows in front of Fairy Glen House. At one stage, the water is carried on a wooden spoot or viaduct, across the burn. David Smith tells me it is a fairly accurate depiction of the system. In the 1950s, David and Douglas Miller dug out the blocked lades, enabling the water to flow once more along the channels. They were successful in filling up one of the pows at the front of Fairy Glen House. The meal mill in Bridge Street also drew on the water from the Rosemarkie burn and Betty's drawing shows the mill lade travelling down to the mill. After use, the water was returned to the burn via a stream that ran along the back of Rose Cottage, but has since been diverted underneath the road. This drawing is not to scale and is drawn from Betty's memory of the Fairy Glen during her holidays here in the 1920s and 30s.

This photo of the pond in the Fairy Glen was taken sometime in the 1940s or 50s. You can clearly see a small island in the centre, Every year a family of mallard ducks nested and raised their young on the island. When the RSPB bought the Fairy Glen they decided to improve the pond by removing the reeds and growth which had begun to choke the pond. Unfortunately, the contractor who was hired to carry out the work was a bit over-enthusiastic and cleared away the island, making our mallard family homeless.

"On August 28th 1788, Kenneth McEiver (sic) of Hawk Hill, residing in Stornoway, sold several parcels of land and tenement, in and around Rosemarkie to Hugh MacLean, tacksman of Craigscorrie." This information was extracted from the register of sasines and is the first indication of the presence of Hugh MacLean in Rosemarkie. Hugh is believed to have built Hawk Hill House. He married Margaret Nicholson and they had three sons, Hugh, Patrick and Malcolm. Hugh (snr) died at Rosemarkie on October 29th 1829 and was buried in Beauly Priory. His son Patrick is commemorated by a wall plaque in Rosemarkie Churchyard. The plaque, which I located behind a holly tree, reads: "Erected by a few friends and neighbours in remembrance of Patrick MacLean of Hawkhill, Captain, Highland Rifle Militia. Nine Years Provost of Fortrose and long resident at Rosemarkie. Died in London July 1864."

In 1879 Hawk Hill House was owned by Charles Arthur Nicholson, who may have been a relative of Hugh MacLean's wife. When it became a hotel, the name was changed to Hawk Hill Marine Hotel. A plaque on the wall next to Miller's Hotel (see page 10) testifies to this. It became the Marine Hotel when it again changed hands.

This photograph of the Marine Hotel probably dates from the 1930s. You can see that extensive alterations have been made to the building. I'm told the tower at the left-hand side was added by Charles Nicholson and the top storey, just behind the tower, was added by Miss McFarlane who owned the hotel from the twenties until the 1960s. The Marine was a popular place for family holidays. During World War II the hotel was requisitioned by the army and used as Army HQ, while two huts were erected on the land at the front of the hotel to accommodate soldiers. It is now run as a nursing home.

Families returned to The Marine Hotel year after year. These photos were taken in 1937 by a member of the family of Ann Robb, who now lives in Fortrose. During the 1930s she and her family made regular visits to the Marine Hotel.

Miller's Hotel was a coaching inn supposed to have been built by two Miller brothers originally from Caithness. The date of the picture is unknown but could be around 1903/4. The lady in black standing in front of the right-hand side window, and wearing the hat, is believed to be Mrs Agnes Gordon, daughter of John Miller and his wife Agnes MacKinnon. Note the plaque on the wall to the left of the building: this is a sign directing people to the Hawk Hill Marine Hotel 100 yards away. It's interesting to note that the building adjoining Miller's Hotel was demolished over a hundred years ago. The gable end is still standing today and looks just as it does in this photograph. The name "Miller's Hotel" is carved into the sandstone lintel above the entrance to the hotel under the arch and as far as I know, it is still there, albeit under a layer of plasterboard.

The photo on the left shows Mr William Miller at the railway station. On the right is Mr Miller dressed in his funeral attire.

Miller's Hotel owned several ponies and traps which they used to transport guests to their hotel. According to Rod Anderson, several travellers came to Miller's Hotel about three or four times a year during the late 19th and early 20th centuries, where they would put up for a few days. Mr Miller would then transport the travellers and their baskets of samples and wares to all the other villages round about the Black Isle where they took orders from the shops and traders. The pony and trap was also used to take guests and their luggage to and from the railway station at Fortrose. Mr Miller also used the trap for weddings and funerals.

Brae House stood at the bottom of The Manse Brae on the site of the present layby and post box. It was demolished in the early 60s when the road was widened. This was the home of the Miller family who owned Miller's Hotel across the road.

Jock Owens and Chris Miller in the kitchen of Brae House. Chris was the mother of Sybil Campbell and grandmother to Valerie MacLennan and Shirley Black.

This is a back view of Ootsey, now known as Mill House. It started life as one of two corn mills in Rosemarkie, and according to Jock Miller, it was built by Mr John Sutherland of Learnie, when he returned to Rosemarkie from India sometime in the 19th century.

In 1907 it was bought by Mr John Robb, who also owned the Plough Inn and a grocer's shop in the High Street. The building was turned into a laundry and during World War I there were 26 workers employed there, 20 of whom were women. The laundry had a contract with the War Office to wash the sheets and blankets from each of the military bases round about the Moray Firth. Mr Robb also employed several carters to collect the laundry which came from Fort George, Cromarty, Invergordon, and Inverness. Laundry from Fort George was shipped across the firth at Chanonry Point and taken by cart to Ootsey.

No doubt there were many private contracts as well as I remember being told that my great-grandfather Colin More, a carter, had a contract to convey the laundry between Rosehaugh House and Ootsey. The sheets and blankets were rinsed in the mill wheel with water from the burn. Rod Anderson talks about going down to the front in the morning and seeing sheets and blankets drying on the grass right along the sea front down as far as the lighthouse. The wee wood at the rear of Ootsie was also used as a drying area with poles and wire covering the whole of the area.

The building was converted to a house sometime in the 1930s.

Street Scenes

A very old photograph of High Street. The man at the door on the extreme right-hand side of the photo is Charlie Junor, grandfather of David Smith and Marion Clelland and father-in-law of Jessie Junor, Fortrose.

This photo of the top end of High Street was taken about 1908. Jeannie Bissett, who was born in 1900, is the girl on the second right of the picture. She's standing outside "Fernlea", the house where she was born. The cottage to the right of the picture was demolished sometime in the 1930s and replaced by two council houses.

Another photograph of High Street, taken probably in the 1940s. The large house on the left with the gable end to the street was called Plane Tree House and has been demolished. The house on the left is called Eilean Donan.

This original photograph is a very early view of Bridge Street. Written in pencil at the bottom right is 1859. This view has a ruined gable end at the bottom of the Kincurdie Drive, and on the wall can be seen fish hanging out to dry. Albion Cottages are on the extreme left. Craigbank Cottage has a wall surrounding it and you can see through the trees as far as Rose Cottage at the top of Bridge Street.

THE VILLAGE, ROSEMARKIE.

Bridge Street about fifty years later. In comparing it with the previous photograph, you will see that the gable end on the right-hand side has been demolished and the wall round Craigbank Cottage has given way to neat railings. Craigbank, (not to be confused with Craigbank Cottage) has been built. Note that the trees have grown considerably in the time between the taking of the two photos, although this photo is taken in summer, the previous one in winter. Craigbank was accidentally burned down by members of the Polish Army who had requisitioned the house during World War II and Rod Anderson, who worked for Kenneth MacRae in the tailor's shop at the rear of the house, was out of a job. He set up his own business in his home in the High Street. The house was never rebuilt and was forever known as The Burnt House.

This is The Gallowbank – Charlie Junor's house on Hawkhill. Charlie owned a market garden on the site and the tumbledown cottage was used to stable his horse and store his equipment, although he was known to have spent the night there himself on a few occasions! He sold the land to the MacIver family in the 1920s or 30s.

The following five postcards were sent to Corporal John Miller by his sister Agnes while he was serving in the Armoured Service Corps in Cape Colony, South Africa. The postmarks on the cards date from October 1905 to August 1908. John Miller obviously enjoyed getting the reminders of his home village as he kept the postcards and they are in remarkably good condition considering they are all over 100 years old. Agnes Miller was Isobel Grigor's great-aunt and lived in Kincurdie Cottage.

An early view of Bridge Street.

AVENUE AT ST HELENA ROSEMARKIE

The avenue of trees shown in this photograph of St Helena no longer exists, although there are a few very old trees which could be the residue of the fabulous planting that Mr Hogarth undertook in the early 1800s. It's not known who the gentleman in the photo is. It's too late for Mr Hogarth and possibly too early for "Crookie." A Mr Nicolson owned the estate in between those two owners

The date stamp on the St Helena postcard is 1908. Originally called Drummarkie, this small estate was, in 1815, in the ownership of a Mr Hogarth, a partner in the firm Messrs Hogarth of Aberdeen. The company owned extensive fishing rights all down the east coast of Scotland. Mr Hogarth renamed the estate St Helena after the island of the same name in the South Atlantic which he is believed to have visited. He also built a well, named it Napoleon's Well and planted willow cuttings taken from a willow tree growing beside Napoleon's grave. In the 1940s a Mr Cruickshanks (known locally as "Crookie") owned the land and the estate name reverted to Drummarkie. Before moving to Drummarkie, Mr Cruickshanks owned the Central Hotel in Avoch, now known as The Harbour Inn.

In 1950 Drummarkie was bought by Herbert Wyllie, who lived in Ardersier but who had local connections. Herbert owned two sawmills in Avoch and Ewenie Clark, together with his brothers James and George and their father Jimmy, all worked there as sawmillers and woodcutters. Herbert's nephew Cameron Wylie and his family moved in to the house at Drummarkie and Ewenie, who was home on leave from the army, was given the job of clearing out the house and making it ready for the family. He opened an old wardrobe in one of the bedrooms and found a row of swallowtail coats hanging there. This conjures up a completely different view of "Crookie" who was a kenspeckle figure in his old age as he wandered about Rosemarkie. White tie dinners, music and fine dining may have been the order of the day at the Central Hotel in its heyday!

Shortly after the family moved in there was a terrific storm and hundreds of trees were blown down in the Fairy Glen. Ewenie's father was given the job of setting up a sawmill on the Drummarkie land to harvest the fallen trees. Mr Clark built a small two-bench sawmill powered by a diesel engine at the head of the Fairy Glen not far from the house. James and his father also built a narrow-gauge railway track from the Fairy Glen up to the main road. A layby was cut into the bank at the side of the road and a tractor-powered winch was constructed to haul the bogey, loaded with trees, up the steep slope. They were then loaded on to a lorry and transported to the sawmill. The trees were cut into different lengths: for pit-props, telegraph poles and railway sleepers, depending on suitability and sent south, usually to Fife, by railway. About a year later, when all the fallen trees were finally removed, the sawmill and the railway were demolished and today there is no sign that they ever existed.

When the Wylie family moved into Drummarkie, the only source of water was Napoleon's Well. The water had to be physically hauled up in a bucket. Jimmy Clark got the job of fitting a Lister engine and pump to the well, which pumped water up to a tank on land above the house. The water then flowed from the tank to the house.

Today, the land surrounding Drummarkie is very over-grown and practically inaccessible. With permission from the present owner, I was able to visit Napoleon's Well. It's now just a hole in the ground, covered in vegetation, and with no sign of the willow trees planted by Mr Hogarth. French terra-cotta tiles, in a surprisingly new condition, are laid in a semi-circle round part of the well, forming a small wall about two feet high. A canopy must have existed at one time and I found fairly large pieces of stained-glass scattered round the well.

The original entrance to Drummarkie was from the Hill of Fortrose, but when a new road was built from the Cromarty Road side, this fell into disuse. A house has now been built over the original road and at a point where a track still exists, a padlocked gate now bars the way.

This card of Marine Terrace is postmarked July 1908. Two substantial buildings, a house and the swimming baths, stand on the land which is now occupied by Crofter's Bistro and the bistro car park. Kincurdie Cottage and Jubilee Cottage are visible, but only the two villas, Firthview and Shandon have been built.

This very clear photo shows the cottage standing on the land at the front of the present Crofter's restaurant and behind it, the Baths.

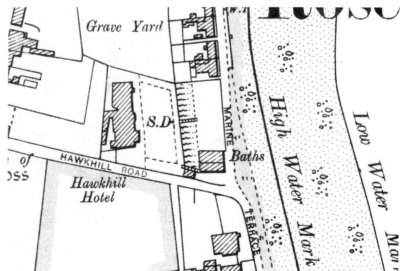

The Ordnance Survey map dated 1904 says simply "Baths". Apparently the water to fill them was pumped up from the sea, presumably when the tide was in!

Map: National Libraries of Scotland

This postcard of The Shore is date-stamped August 1906. The black shed could be the site of a boat-building and repair business. The iron railings round the wall of the Marine Hotel are visible here, but they were removed in 1940 when the Government requisitioned all 19th century iron railings and gates to be used to build aeroplanes for the war effort.

According to the Ordnance Survery map on the facing page, drawn in connection with electoral boundaries in 1832 at the time of the Great Reform Act, a ropery stood on the north side of the burn, on the edge of the present-day playing field. A hundred years later, Alistair Fraser in his booklet "Random Notes on Old Rosemarkie" places a ropery in the area between Jubilee Cottage and the road.

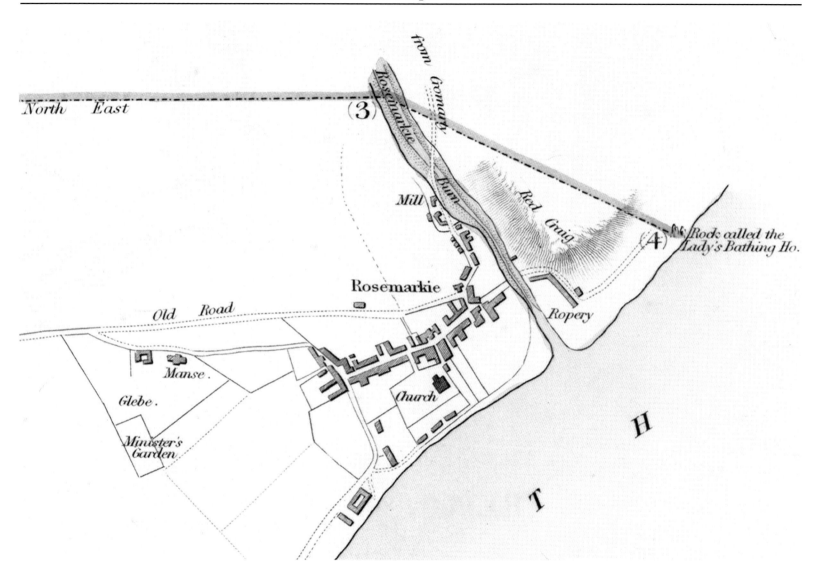

North East

from Gomary

Rosemarkie

(3)

Mill

Burn

Red Craig

(4)

Rock called the
Lady's Bathing Ho.

Rosemarkie

Old Road

Manse.

Ropery

Glebe.

Church

Minister's
Garden

H

T

This picture of the old Meal Mill in Bridge Street was probably taken at around the same time as the photo of Bridge Street on Page 21. It looks pretty dilapidated, but apparently it was a working mill until 1939 when it closed. Mr MacRae was the last miller. The farmers carted their oats to the mill for milling, then collected the meal later. They also collected the bran which was used for pig feed. In this picture, a horse and cart can be seen standing at a flight of steps and the miller is carrying a bag of meal to be loaded on to the cart.

Clifton House site

Tom More's garden

Cloy Cottage

Miss MacGregor, Newsagent

Mrs MacAndrew's post office and shop

Albion Cottages

Cottage where Neil MacIntosh lived

ROSEMARKIE LOOKING W. 20313 JV

This photograph is believed to be pre-1896. A ruin stands on the site of Clifton House which was built in 1896. The Gordon Memorial Hall has not yet been built. The buildings around the Plough Inn are intact and Cloy Cottage stands at the bottom of the High Street, where the telephone box and post pillar now stand. Also visible are Albion Cottages, at the foot of Courthill Road. Miss MacGregor had a newsagents business in the left-hand part of Albion Cottages, but this was not until well into the 1900s. Note that there is a building in between the Plough Inn and Seafield. This is the building where Mrs Jeannie MacAndrew ran her post office and grocery. The present pub restaurant was a substantial cottage in 1908, and in the 40s and 50s when The Plough was owned by Neil MacIntosh, he and his wife lived there. Two cottages stand in the grassed area beside the Plough Inn. Note the open ground where the car park now stands. During the 40s I remember my great-uncle Tom More having a vegetable garden there.

Shops

Mr John Robb ran a grocer's shop at the bottom of the High Street in the early 1900s. He bought and rebuilt the Plough Inn and was responsible for turning the corn mill (Ootsey) into a laundry in1907.

Sometime in the 1920s or 30s Daniel Fraser took over the grocer's shop previously run by Mr Robb. This is the shop that I remember going to for my mother's messages in the 40s when I was four years old. I would hand over my list and Daniel would fill my bag. I loved the smell of the shop and the fact that the shelves went right up to the ceiling. I lived in the Ness Croft, now called Scorrielea, and I walked to Rosemarkie and back through a field of cows and horses. I never came to any harm and apparently I did this journey regularly.

This method of shopping, which was still in existence in the middle 60s, was that you "marked" your purchases and paid for them at the end of the month when you got paid. My mother had a little book just like this in which she wrote her list and Daniel put the price next to the item. Mrs MacPherson-Davidson, resident in Ootsey, was doing the same thing back in 1936.

H. HOME. Rosemarkie.

The shop and house at the rear, 12 and 14 High Street, were built by John Carpenter Steavenson, a general merchant who was Provost of Fortrose in 1837. Later, Hugh Home ran it as a general store and Post Office. Mrs Annie Rennie and her sister Ella, who lived in the High Street, Fortrose, were daughters of Mr Home. I remember both these ladies in the 1950s when I worked as a shop assistant in the Co-op in the High Street in Fortrose. Annie Rennie died in September 1968, and she could be the little girl in the photo. Betty Forrester's father, Robert Ross worked as a message boy in the shop. One day a customer came in asking for mint. Robert was sent down to the Rosemarkie burn to gather some wild mint which Mr Home duly sold to his customer. When Mr Home gave up the business, the Post Office moved to a building next to the Plough Inn and was run by Mrs Jeannie MacAndrew, while Miss Mary MacGillivray took over the shop. After this the SCWS occupied the shop and this was followed by K. Cumming and Son, Butchers. It is now used as a private residence.

In 1913 Miss Mary MacGillivray heard that the grocer's shop at 12 High Street, Rosemarkie was up for sale, so she cycled from Bogroy, where her parents owned the Bogroy Inn, to check it out. It was obviously to her liking, because Mary bought the business. This was probably when Hugh Home retired.

Mary brought an assistant with her by name of Lizzie and for almost a year, Mary and Lizzie slept in a room at the rear of the shop until Mary rented East Court, 11 High Street a year later. When she eventually bought the property, Mary renamed the house Tigh an Aigh, and this is where her niece, Susan Seright now lives.

The only thing that was sold from this shop, was ice-cream, which Susan's granny sold during the summer, although Mary may have used the shop windows to display goods from her shop across the road.

Tigh an Aigh was built as a shop and private dwelling but had a bakehouse at the rear. This consisted of a huge oven and a workshop for preparing the dough. The bakery was never in production. The builder went bankrupt in 1900 just as the building was completed and the project was taken over by the bank. It was then sold to a Mr James Fraser, baker, 27 High Street, Fortrose. Mr Fraser already owned a bakery business in Fortrose and he refused to allow anyone to run a bakery business from the building.

The bakery has since been connected to the main house and converted to a living space, The bricks from the oven, all in pristine condition, have been used to pave an area at the rear of the house.

Photo, back: Isabel Gordon; left: Mary MacGillivrey with Lizzie and Jimmy Lumsden.

Jimmy Lumsden worked for Mary as a delivery boy and he is pictured above with his delivery bike. I'm told that the shop had no set hours and was known to stay open on occasion until midnight. Mary continued to run her grocer's shop until she retired in 1944 when the shop was taken over by the SCWS. I remember shopping there in the late 1940s or early 50s when Irene Smith from Fortrose, who went on to marry Jimmy Lumsden, worked there as a shop assistant. Kenneth A MacRae, writing in his book, "Highland Doorstep", says Mary MacGillivray told him that after thirty years in business, she was still regarded as an incomer in Rosemarkie.

Lewie and Jane Grant.

This is a modern view of Rosemarkie High Street and the only photo I could find showing Lewie Grant's shop. This picture was taken in 1965. The High Street looks much the same today as it did then. The people in the street are Beelack MacAndrew, Isobel MacNeil and Robert More.

Lewie Grant and his grocer's van.

The picture on the left is a page from the 1947 ledger showing all cheques paid out by Lewie Grant. The ledger entry dated April 3rd shows a cheque made out to M. Grigor. Mark Grigor set snares every night on his father's farm, The Corslet. He checked them every morning and handed in any rabbits caught to Lewie Grant before going on to Fortrose Academy. In the picture on the right we have a ledger page showing the goods Lewie bought in and the price paid. Mark must have been pretty good at setting the snares as he supplied Lewie with rabbits every day except Sunday.

Unknown, Ivy Gordon,
Sandy Gordon, Caroline
Anderson, Isabel
Gordon, Mary
MacGillivray, Sybil
Miller.

This group is standing outside the Post Office at 9 High Street, sometime in the 1930s. When Mrs Jeannie MacAndrew, who ran the Post Office next to the Plough Inn left in 1935/36 to look after the family of her brother Daniel MacIver who had been widowed, a Mrs Fraser took over the shop but not the Post Office, so George and Mabel Fraser set up the Post Office in the family home. George, who had been gassed in World War I, ran an ironmonger's shop in the building across the road where Crofter Foods now stands. I remember the Post Office in the 40s and 50s when it was run by Mabel. It was a dark place as she didn't believe in wasting electricity, but it was also a pleasant place to go because Mabel was very good at handing out sweeties .

Rosemarkie Post Office

Rosemarkie Beach

The tennis courts and bathing huts from the beach after 1923. The large rock on the centre right of the photo is the rock known as The Ladies' Bathing House.

The Cunnack (pictured): this stone lies about 100 yards out to sea in front of the tennis courts. When I was young we used to dive and jump off it and it seemed pretty high then. Nowadays, it looks rather small, not more than about four feet high. Some years ago I read an article which called this stone The Cunny Stone. I have no idea where the name came from or what it means, but it has always been known as The Cunnack. Rosemarkie people have a habit of adding "ack" to many words and names, a practice popular in the Black Isle. For example we have "Beelack" (Bill), "Jeemack" (Jim) and "Deedack" (David).

The Tubback: another landmark on Rosemarkie beach, looks pretty ordinary from the land, but when the tide is out you can get to the sea side of it and you will see how it got its name. The rock has been eroded away by the constant movement of the sea to form a tub-like cave. It is partly open at the top and when there's a rough sea you can hear the boom of the waves in the cavern, or "tub." The spray being forced out through the narrow opening on the top can be quite spectacular.

The Stile: If you walk further along the path, you come to The Stile. It's a bit of a misnomer as there is no stile there now. There was once a fence that stretched down across the path on to the beach and this is where the stile was built. It eventually fell apart and when new fences were erected, the path was left clear with no further need of a stile. Rosemarkie people still refer to that point as "the stile".

The Grazings: this is the area of grass which stretches from the stile to the first cave and was once common grazing land. My father told me that when he was a boy he drove a cow belonging to Mrs Ross, Courthill Smiddy, over to the grazings every morning before going to school. He brought it back after school.

This postcard was sent to Corporal J Miller in Cape Colony by K Holm. The caption says "Devines Cave, Rosemarkie" and handwritten below, "the girl is the maid in Kincurdy." The Devine's didn't actually live in a cave, but in a "bender", a traditional traveller's tent built of bent branches and covered in tarpaulins or turf, beside Cairds cave. Mr Devine mended pots and pans and sharpened knives and scissors. Sometime in the early 1920s the couple moved to Chanonry Point, where they erected their bender beside a tumbledown cottage next to the ice house. Local people looked after the Devines, as they did other travelling people, giving them food and clothing. Jean MacArthur's mother delivered milk to the Devines all the way from Lambton Farm and Isobel Grigor's aunts, Nettie and Jessie Young, delivered milk to the Devines at the Ness. The Parish Council became concerned about the health and living conditions of the Devines, so they closed down their home and placed them in the poorhouse.

Wild and Free

I love my home, 'tis wild and free
No culture does it need.
God placed it there, there let it stand
Fashioned by His Mighty Hand
And a gift to Adam's seed.
No spot upon this rock-bound coast
Such a lovely stretch of beach can boast
As seen at Flowerburn.
Where wild flowers bloom the whole year round
And lovely hybridous plants are found
In rocky glen and burn.

The Ferry Ford – 'tis wild and free
Washed and cleaned each day
The hand of man has not yet marred
This ancient relic – made by the Lord
Nor stopped the right of way.
The landmarks that for centuries stood
The fiercest shock of wind and flood
Keep nobly to the post.
Green sentinels they, Oh, could they speak
The story told would blanch the cheek
Of lives and shipping lost.

The Ferry Cove – 'tis wild and free
Dame Nature placed it there.
Her throne, the rocky dome above
Beneath – the redbreast and the dove
Each morning for a mate.
The crystal pendants – has no charm for them
For, lying beside that fallen stem
Upon Dame Nature's bed.
The waving frond of a frozen fern
As if to ward off further harm
Beneath both mates lie dead.

The Murry Firth, 'tis wild and free
He laughs at the coming storm
Tho' the wild winds whistle, what cares he
He knows the track where the harvesters be
Must keep my boats from harm.
I'll first have a look around by Nairn
Call at the tail of the bank and learn
What's become of the fleet.
They all know me and I know them too,
To be dodging like this, the thing won't do,
Causes their wives to greet.

Composed by King Fern (William Devine) Rosemarkie

This poem was taken from "Rosemarkie, A Village History", a book compiled by Rosemarkie WRI in 1966 as their entry into a competition by the SWRI Federation to celebrate 75 years of the Association. It's not great poetry, but I thought I would include it in this book as it gives another slant to the life of William Devine. Apparently he called himself "Captain" Devine, but I can find no trace of any military or naval records for him. Nor can I find any trace of his death.

These are the rocks at "The Ferry" which Mr Devine calls "the ferry ford" in his poem. At high tide there is no access further along the beach. Metal rings were attached to the rocks and strung with ropes to form a bridge to be used by the salmon fishermen to cross safely if they were caught by the incoming tide. According to the late Sandy Jack, there were two rows of metal rings and ropes, one a few feet above the other. The men walked along the bottom rope and held on to the top rope. Sometime in the 1970s or 80s, I remember seeing a new rope inserted in the metal rings. It didn't last long however, and soon rotted away, presumably by the constant immersion in the salt water.

Chanonry Ferry

There was a ferry at Chanonry Point for centuries, when pilgrims and travellers, businessmen and merchants, crossed the short distance to make their way further afield. The crossing was part of the pilgrims' way and was used by King James IV when he travelled on pilgrimage to the shrine of St Duthac in Tain.

In 1939 Alex MacLean, the ferryman, (pictured with his sister outside the ferryhouse) was drowned and the ferry ceased.

In the 18th and early 19th centuries, salmon fishing was an important industry in Rosemarkie and Chanonry Point was crucial to its success. There were several fishing stations between Chanonry Point and Eathie and bothies were situated along the coast to accommodate the fishermen during the salmon fishing season which was from February to July. The salmon was packed in ice and carried down to the pier at Chanonry Point. Here it was loaded on to a passenger steamer which plied between Inverness and London, and conveyed to Billingsgate market. There was also a fairly large passenger traffic from Chanonry Point with people joining the steamer at Chanonry rather than travel all the way to Inverness.

I came across the following article printed in the Inverness Advertiser, on Friday February 3rd 1871:

"Proposed Branch Railway to Fort George

We are glad to learn that this proposal which was agitated in our columns some months ago, has been revived in a direction from which some practical result may be expected. A meeting was held at Fortrose on Monday to consider the subject; and a deputation consisting of the magistrates of the burgh and several other gentlemen had a conference afterwards with Mr Mackintosh of Raigmore, MP. Although the proposal is in the very earliest stage at present, it is gratifying to learn that as a practicable scheme it has taken a firm hold on the minds of the leading merchants and agriculturists in the Black Isle and the Ardersier district. The cost of such a branch line, from 'Fort George Station' – sadly misnamed – to the Fort and ferry, would be comparatively small, while the passenger and goods traffic would be considerable. We are sure the Black Isle proprietors would subscribe heartily to this short and economical line, a branch from the Muir of Ord being now considered impracticable on account of the enormous expense. Were the assistance and co-operation of the Government secured by the permanent settlement at Fort George of a regiment of the regular service, the scheme could not fail to be a financial success. Why do not the Town Councils of the northern burghs take this in hand and memorialise the Secretary of War on the subject. When a more equitable distribution over the country of the national forces is being everywhere discussed, no time could be more suitable for the purpose."

Who knows, we may have had the Chanonry Bridge, rather than the Kessock Bridge if this proposal had gone ahead!

219, GALLOWGATE,

Aberdeen, January 18th 1861

Mr Thomas Gordon

Rosemarkie

BOUGHT OF W. ROUTLEDGE & SON,

Manufacturers of all sorts of Rope and Twine,

Salmon, Bag, and Fly Nets, Fishing Lines, Dressed Hemp and Flax, Grain Sacks, Sheep Flake Netting, &c. &c.

Thomas Gordon was heavily involved in the salmon fishing industry and when I was looking for proof that steamers did indeed stop at Chanonry Point, I found these receipts from W Routledge and Son of Aberdeen and the North of Scotland Steam Shipping Co., both calling at Chanonry Point.

On checking the Inverness Advertiser between 1820 and 1850, I found that there were several shipping companies operating vessels between Inverness, Aberdeen, Edinburgh and London, carrying freight, livestock and passengers.

The Freight and Charges hereon are payable when the goods are landed from the Steamer.

CHANONRY POINT, 13th April 186 3

To The North of Scotland Steam Shipping Co.

G. Paulin, Agent.

Events

The laying of the foundation stone of the Gordon Memorial Hall

The Gordon Memorial Hall was built in 1904, and legend has it that it was funded by two sisters from Miller's Hotel, to commemorate their husbands, two brothers with the surname Gordon. They were Isabella Miller who married Thomas Gordon and Agnes, married to John Gordon. Thomas died on December 20th 1897 and John died on February 10th 1903. According to the following report in the Ross shire Journal, Mr John Gordon alone was responsible for funding the building of the hall. The foundation stone was laid on Thursday March 31st 1904, and on Tuesday August 16th that same year the hall was officially opened by Mr Fletcher, Rosehaugh.

Report from the Ross shire Journal, dated Friday April 8th 1904:
"The town of Rosemarkie was en fete last Thursday to celebrate the ceremony of laying the foundation stone of the Gordon Memorial Hall there. The hall is a gift from Mr Gordon, Rosemarkie, a gentleman who took a very warm interest in all that appertained to the good of the burgh, and who had often expressed a wish to see a suitable hall built in Rosemarkie which could be used as a reading room and library, and be serviceable for all public functions, and Mrs Gordon is now giving expression to this by giving the hall to the inhabitants, and it is understood that the building will be vested with the Town Council of Fortrose as trustees. The site is a very pretty one, and when finished the hall will be a great ornament to the place, besides being a great public benefit. The ceremony took place amidst much enthusiasm. A procession was formed at the United Free Hall, and marched to the site. It was headed by pipers and marshalled by ex-Baillie Hossack, convenor of the Building Committee: and consisted of the school children from Rosemarkie Public School, the Provost, Magistrates, and Town Council of Fortrose, the members of the Building Committee and the general public of whom there was a large gathering. Provost Geddie was asked to preside, and after a prayer by Rev. J Macdowall, he in the name of the committee, presented a very handsome silver trowel, with suitable inscription, to Mrs Gordon and asked her to perform the ceremony of laying the foundation stone. This was very gracefully performed by the lady donor, and on the call of Mr Gillanders, who spoke in very high terms of what had been done by Mr and Mrs Gordon for the town, and especially of the present magnificent gift, a most hearty vote of thanks was given, cheer following upon cheer. Various other speeches of a complimentary character were made. Rev. J Macdowall replied in the name of Mrs Gordon. After the ceremony a cake and wine banquet was served in Miss Miller's hotel at the cross."

I'm told the silver trowel is now in the possession of the "Miller Trust".

From the Ross shire Journal, Friday August 19th 1904
"Gordon Memorial Hall – This hall was opened to the public on Tuesday. A large gathering collected in front of the Hall about noon, when a silver key was presented to Mr Fletcher of Rosehaugh, who opened the door and formally declared the Hall opened. A cake and wine banquet was held in the Hall. Provost Geddie proposed the health of the donor, Mrs Gordon, Rosemarkie, who, he said, had carried out a wish expressed by her husband, Baillie Gordon, but that this was only one of the many kindnesses on her part, and that time after time the community had been indebted to Mrs Gordon and her late husband for generous deeds. In the evening a concert was given, the whole programme being supplied by visitors."

The opening of the Gordon Memorial Hall by Mr Fletcher, Rosehaugh. The lady on the right hand side of the door is Mrs Agnes Gordon and next to her is her sister, Isabella. Mr Fletcher is the gentleman in the tweed coat and the gentleman in the tall hat is probably Provost Geddie.

During both world wars, a canteen was set up in the hall to cater for the many soldiers stationed in and around Rosemarkie. It was staffed by local volunteers and I was told by the late Willie Miller that the ladies were adept at making a little go a long way. Today the hall is administered by a local committee and is used almost to capacity by local groups and others.

This is the grand opening of the tennis courts in 1923 and shows people at play with a celebration of sorts going on in the background. In the 1920s things were arranged exactly the same as they are today: a committee of local people negotiated with the Rosehaugh Estate for the lease of the land at the beach and raised funds to pay for the building of the courts. The wood used to build the intricate fencing round the courts was cut from the Kincurdie Estate.

The tennis courts were well used and tournaments were arranged every Thursday afternoon during the summer between locals and visitors from both the Marine Hotel and the Marita Boarding house. It was a very social occasion, with the Rosemarkie ladies preparing afternoon teas for everyone taking part. Sandy Hossack had a rowing boat and took people out for trips round the bay for sixpence a time. Today the tennis courts have fallen into disrepair and the Rosemarkie Amenities Association has begun fund-raising to bring them back to an acceptable standard.

This photo is probably of the local committee who raised the money to build the tennis courts. Back row: no one is identified. Middle, from left: Glad MacIver, Min Ross, Nell Holm (sister of Maggie), Mrs Jack (mother of Jenny Paterson), Mrs Denoon (grandmother of Ian Basham), Jess MacKenzie (grandmother of Hugh MacKenzie), Kate Bissett, Miss Reid (teacher at Rosemarkie School), Bella Sinclair (Muirhead) the twin sister of Mary MacIver. Front: third left is Miss MacGillivray then John Hossack (Tigh na Mara). The next lady is unidentified. Next is Provost Willie Gillanders and Mrs Mary MacIver, Greenside Farm. The boy at the extreme right and the two people with the horse have not been identified.

The ancient game of bools was revived in 1955 to celebrate the quincentenery of Fortrose receiving its Royal Charter. The result on this occasion was a draw.

First left is Jimmy Ross, father of Cathie Garrow and Margaret Noble; third from left is Malcolm Morrison then Hugh More, Derek Anderson, Billy Hossack, Robert More, Roddy Shaw (behind Robert), Dr John Anderson holding trophy, John Anderson, Mrs Anderson, Fred Fraser, Ephie Sinclair, Sandy Hossack, Rod Anderson, Jimmy MacFarlane, Eck Ross, Charlie MacKenzie, Mr Rowat (of Rowat's Tea and who lived in Firthview), Jock Bain, George Junor, Hugh MacKenzie, Willie Miller. Front: Ken Urquhart, Willie Taylor and Dodo Wilson.

"Bools is an ancient game that was played on New Year's day between teams from Fortrose and Rosemarkie. The game is played by four teams, two starting from Fortrose and two from Rosemarkie. Each team has a round ball about the size of a tennis ball and weighing about four pounds. The balls are thrown by the teams to a meeting point at the Brahan Seer stone, near the 18th hole, on the golf course. At the stone, the two teams from each place join forces and compete against each other at throwing the bools to Peterson's Dyke and back."

This was how the game of bools was described in the publicity in 1955. The Brahan Seer stone is the original stone which lies in the whins at the front of the clubhouse, and is well known to the people of Fortrose and Rosemarkie. Peterson's Dyke presented me with a challenge. After asking several residents of Rosemarkie, Isobel Grigor came up with the answer. Some years ago her aunt, Jessie Young was asked by the golf club to write a brief history of the events leading to the formation of the Club in 1888.

The sub-committee formed to deal with the proprietors and tenants of the land through which the golf course would pass identified several owners of land and in November 1889, after the successful negotiation for purchase or rental of several pieces of land, the shaping of the golf course began. Apparently all the land towards Chanonry Point was divided into feus and owned by various people, such as John Smith, Fortrose, John Home, Rosemarkie, D. Ross, Chanonry Point, Kenneth MacKenzie, Courthill, Rosemarkie and Alexander (Sandy) Paterson, the Pilk, Fortrose. They all agreed to sell or rent. Sandy Paterson sold his piece of land for £100. It would appear that Sandy Paterson's piece of land was situated where the second putting green now stands and contained a long ridge extending almost to the road. Jessie Young remembers calling this ridge "Sandy Paterson's Dyke." So, we have the correct name: Paterson's, not Peterson's, Dyke. It is interesting to note that the second hole on the present layout of the golf course, is called "The Dyke".

It was a very sore point with the golfers that the route for the carts carrying ice from the pows down to the ice-house at Chanonry Point continued on their hereditary route over the newly prepared putting greens. The golf club complained to the Town Council, but they took no action as they did not wish to interfere with "the liberties of the public"! Apparently a new road was constructed eventually.

Another event during the Fortrose Quincentenery celebrations was the Beating of the Bounds, when a group of Fortrose and Rosemarkie youth walked the boundaries of the parish. The ceremony is an old one which used to be enacted once a year to ensure that the boundaries of the parish were known to the residents and the information passed down through the generations. On this occasion the participants were Ian Basham, Murdo MacPhail, Douglas Miller and William Jack, shown here with Dr John Anderson. Note the sign behind them. Fortrose Town Council erected this sign at the west end of Rosemarkie, just at the top of Bridge Street. It wasn't there for long, however, as it mysteriously disappeared one night and was found a few days later lying in the Rosemarkie Burn. The council erected another one, but the Rosemarkie people had made their point.

On The Buses

In 1912 Mr Hastie introduced a bus service betwcen Cromarty and Kessock Ferry.

During the 20 years just before and after World War II, "the buses" was a favourite form of employment for Rosemarkie men and women. Alec and Ken MacKenzie, Fred Fraser, Willie MacKenzie and John Smith, all went on to marry local girls, some of them bus conductresses. No fewer than seven drivers and ten conductresses lived in Rosemarkie. Mary Gallie always wore the white uniform in the summer months. This dress was discontinued after World War II but Mary held on to hers and wore it between May 1st and September 30th every year.

Clockwise from top left: A Highland Bus; Alec "The Lairdie" MacKenzie; Hattie Sinclair; Mary Gallie in her "whites" with Fred Fraser.

Clockwise from top left: Brother and sister George and Mary Gallie; Alec MacKenzie and John Smith outside the Bus Garage at the top of Ness Road, Fortrose; Dorothy MacLennan, John Smith, Mary MacLean, Willie Taylor; Alec MacKenzie and Mary Gallie in her "whites."

Families

This is the More family, c1916, who lived at 5 Bridge Street, Rosemarkie. Colin More and his wife Christina are seated, with their son, Tom, standing back left, next to Sophia, then Robert who was home on leave from the first world war, and Isabella. Margaret, daughter of Sophia, sits on her grandfather's knee and my father, Freddy Bassindale, son of Isabella, sits on his granny's knee. In the middle at the front is Colin More, youngest son of Colin and Christina.. This was the first time I'd seen an image of my great-grandfather. This photo is in a bad state of repair as it was found in a shed in Fortrose, eaten by wood-worm.

This is the family of Ian Basham, c1908, at the door of Holly Cottage, Bridge Street. John Denoon is Ian's Grandfather. In this photograph, John Denoon stands next to his wife, Mary. He is holding their son, Donald, born 1907. Next to Mary is her mother, also called Mary. The lady at the front, wearing a tippet (shawl) is the baby's great grandmother, Flora Hossack (nee Munro) who died on March 13th 1910 aged 92.

John Denoon was a flesher (butcher) who operated a "killing hoose" (abattoir) in a rear extension to Holly Cottage. He also kept two milking cows and bought up the grass cut from the grazing areas at the beach. In the mid to late 19th century, John's father Donald Denoon kept an inn at the house, one of several in Rosemarkie at the time.

John and Mary Denoon and Mary's mother in the vegetable garden opposite Holly Cottage.

When John Denoon died on February 4th 1942 he was the last surviving Rosemarkie Veteran of the 1st Inverness Highland Volunteers who had attended Queen Victoria's "Wet Review". This was the Royal Review of 39,473 Volunteer Riflemen (later the Territorial Army) that took place in torrential rain in Holyrood Park, Edinburgh on August 25th 1881. It was called the Royal Volunteer Review, but due to the downpour of rain all day, during which the volunteers became completely soaked, with white pipe clay from their belts mingling with the red dye from their tunics, it became known as the "Wet Review". McGonagall commemorated the event in his poem "The Royal Review" and mentions the Inverness Highland Volunteers.

Robert Miller, Plumber and Salmon Fisher, c1916 with his wife Annie and their children, Kitch, Willie (father of Isobel Grigor and Moira Strachan) and Betty outside the cottage on Marine Terrace, where Isobel now lives. Robert and Annie were first cousins, the grandchildren of John Miller and Agnes McKinnon, of Miller's Hotel.

The Fraser family – At the front of the photo on the left is Janet Fraser (nee MacIver), mother of Jeannie, George and Daniel and grandmother of Jenny Paterson. Daniel is in the uniform of the Seaforth Highlanders and George is holding an un-named child. Right: Jeannie Fraser (Jenny Paterson's mother) and Jeannie Bissett, who were cousins.

Mr and Mrs Roddy Gallie, who lived at 11 High Street, now renumbered 25. In the 1940s Roddy Gallie ran a market garden in Courthill Road, beside the Gordon Memorial Hall. He supplied the Marine Hotel and local people with vegetables. I remember, as a young girl, going with my great-granny to buy vegetables from him.

Above: Roddy Gallie's market garden.

Mary and Sandy MacIver of Greenside Farm on their Golden Wedding in February 1930. They were married in Rosemarkie on February 13th 1880 when Mary was 19 and Sandy 23. Sandy is described in the marriage certificate as a ploughman and Mary is a domestic servant. They had 14 children and Sandy became a successful farmer at Greenside. They both lived to celebrate their 70th wedding anniversary in 1950.

The Sinclair Family – Back, from left: Ephraim, Janet, Elsie-Cameron, Ellen, David, Margaret, James; middle: Jean, John Thomas Munro (father of Margaret), Margaret (Munro), Ephraim Sinclair; front: Harriet (mother of Pearl Sinclair), Georgina, Elizabeth MacKenzie (daughter of Ellen and William MacKenzie). Agnes (Adie, daughter of Ellen).

Lilac House, the house on the extreme right, was the home of William and Christina Home, the parents of Maggie Home and grandparents of Lorna Haines. They are the couple on the right. William was a carpenter and undertaker and ran his business from the shop at the front of the house, the steps to which can be seen at the right hand bottom corner. Note the sign above the shop window on the left of the picture. On the original photograph I can make out the name "A Fraser" on the sign. There is a picture of a woman on the window, but it is impossible to tell from this what was sold in the shop.

Minnie Gray, whose name is pencilled on the back of the photograph, ran a bakery in Church Place. Perhaps she worked for A Fraser. On the back of the photo it says "Ina's door, Bella Fraser". Ina Bissett lived in the cottage on the far side of Church Lane and Bella Fraser could be the woman standing at the door.

"Sutherland, Ealing's father" is also mentioned. This could mean that the gent on the left is Mr Sutherland of Balmungie House who had a daughter Eileen. "Ealing" is what I would call a Rosemarkie pronunciation of Eileen. "Mrs Jack's dau., and Nell" are also mentioned. Nell will be Nell Home, daughter of William and Christina.

William
Home and
Christina
Home,
grandparents
of Lorna
Haines,

Miney (Mrs Smith) and Mrs MacDonald, Springwell, who were sisters.

Schooldays

This photograph, taken c1868 at the front of the Schoolhouse, must be one of the earliest photos of Rosemarkie School, which opened sometime in the 1860s. Note the bare feet of some of the pupils at the front. There are 47 pupils in this photo. The twins at the right front of the photo are, I believe, Mary and Bella Anderson. Although they were born at Shoremill in the Parish of Resolis, the family is recorded in the 1871 census as living in Rosemarkie where their father, Alexander Anderson, gives his occupation as a miller. Mary went on to become Mrs Sandy MacIver of Greenside and Bella became Mrs Sinclair, Muirhead.

Rosemarkie School, possibly in 1909 or 10. Jeannie Bisset is the girl on the far left of the third row from the back and her sister Kate is fourth from left in the same row. The girl at the right-hand side of the third row could be Isobel MacIver, daughter of Sandy and Mary, Greenside. Donnie Bisset is first on the left of the front row.

This photograph was taken at the front of Firthview, Marine Terrace, in 1911 or 12. I had great difficulty identifying the location of this photo but, after visiting all the large villas in Rosemarkie, identified it as Firthview. Jeannie Bisset is the girl with white ribbons and white blouse standing to the right of the teacher and Kate Bisset is third from left in the middle row.

Rosemarkie School c1920 – Teachers: Miss Reid on the left and Miss Cheyne on the right. Back row: fourth left, Charlie Robb (Plough Inn); sixth left Willie Denoon. Middle, from left: unknown, unknown, Mary Denoon, unknown, Bobby Owens, Ephraim Sinclair, Hugh MacLeman. Front: unknown, Jessie MacKenzie (Whitebog), Jessie Moir, Bernice Junor, unknown, Mary Ann MacKenzie (Raddery Smiddy), unknown, unknown. Seated at front: unknown, Willie Miller.

Rosemarkie School c1921 – Back row: the teachers are Miss Reid (left) and Miss Cheyne. Freddy Bassindale stands next to Miss Reid. Third row: eighth left, Margaret MacDonald. Second row: fifth left, Caroline Anderson then Mary Gallie, Pheme Urquhart and Florrie Ross. Front: second left, Ken Urquhart.

Rosemarkie School, late 20s – The teacher could be Miss Fraser or Miss Melville. Maggie Jean MacLennan is in the striped cardigan; Ken Urquhart is third left, back row. Middle row, eighth from left, is Marie MacIver, then Pearl Sinclair. John Anderson is in the front row, third from right.

Rosemarkie School, 1920s – back row: first left, Roddy Doddy; second left, Jack (Tulip) Miller; fifth left, Sandy Jack. Third row: extreme left, Rhoda Anderson then Peggy Grove; seventh left, Martha Grieve; eighth left, Babs Miller. Second row: second left, Ella Bews; third right, Jean Miller. Front: first left, Tommy Stott; second left, John Anderson,

Rosemarkie School, 1920s – back, from left: teacher Miss Reid, Jack Grigor (Balmungie), George Gallie, unknown, Willie Grigor (Balmungie), Kenny Munro (Flowerburn), George Anderson (Cloy); the next two boys and the teacher are unknown. Third row: fourth left, Mary MacIver (mother of Fiona Jack and Ali-George Fraser) then Elma MacLean (Flowerburn), Caroline Anderson, Isobel MacKinnon, Katie Grigor, Mary Gallie; the two girls at the end are unknown. Second row: first left, Pearl Sinclair; second left, Adra Munro (Flowerburn); third right, Pheme Urquhart. Front: second left, Sandy Jack; third left, John Anderson; extreme right, Kitch Miller.

Weddings

The wedding of George Fraser and Mabel Anderson c1930 – back, from left: Sandy MacIver (Greenside); Jessie Young; Sandy Anderson (father of the bride); Maggie Bissett; Jean-Ann Anderson; unknown; Mary MacIver (Greenside); Daniel Fraser; Mrs Fraser (mother of the groom); bridesmaid Mary Anderson (niece of the bride); bride Mabel Anderson; Mrs Bissett; groom George Fraser; Mrs MacKay (who ran the Poorhouse); the gentleman just behind Mrs MacKay could be her husband; Rod Anderson; in front of Rod Anderson is Jeannie Jack. Behind the bride is Critessie MacKay and the lady next her is Pen Junor. At the front first right is Jim Anderson, brother of the bride and Ken Jack. Flower-girls are Jenny Jack (Paterson) and Rhoda Anderson and the boys at the front are Sandy Jack (left) and John Anderson.

Violet MacIver, Greenside Farm, and Donald Barlow were married in Rosemarkie Church in 1934. Pictured are their bridesmaids, Marie MacKenzie, Marie MacIver, Rita MacKenzie.

This is the wedding of Johan Ross and Albert Henry Barnes, 1929 or 1930. They were married in the Rosemarkie Parish Church and held the reception in Ross's Tearoom.

In this photo, from left to right are: unknown; Artie Ross (became Mrs D. Lumsden); Helen MacLennan (became Mrs Geddes); unknown; best man; Eileen Sutherland; bridesmaid Lizzie MacLennan; groom Albert Henry Barnes; bride Johan Ross; gent in soft hat is John Ross, father of the bride; unknown; Nell Ross, sister of the bride; Rev Masterton; unknown; Bob Owens. Kneeling at the front, from left: Rod MacKenzie (husband of Ina); Roy MacKenzie; Roy's brother George (Jeej) and Kenny MacLennan (father of Okain MacLennan).

Johan Ross began working in the laundry at Rosehaugh House and later became a lady's maid there. When Miss Elford of Rosehaugh was setting up home in London she asked Johan to move with her and Johan became her personal lady's maid. Johan went on to become an accomplished seamstress. She also played the violin and enjoyed playing for her employer on occasion.

Nell Ross owned the tearooms in the High Street and during World War II it was a favourite place for the troops to meet.

George Gallie and Gina MacLeman married on 12th June 1945, three weeks after George came home from the war. Best man was Ken Urquhart and bridesmaid was Mary Gallie

Donald Galllie and Jessie MacRae.

The wedding of Mary Gallie and Willie MacKenzie in Rosemarkie Church.

Wedding of Sybil Millar and Dodo Campbell. Sybil is a direct descendant of the Miller family who owned Miller's Hotel. Her daughters Valerie and Shirley live in Inverness and Elgin respectively. The bridesmaids are Mary Gallie and Jessie Johnstone who went on to marry Jack Junor, Rosemarkie.

Groups

According to the information attached to this photograph, it was taken in Church Lane. There is no date, but note the ruined wall to the left of the picture. Mrs Cameron and Mrs More are the two ladies on the front left, and these will be my great-granny Christina More and her sister Margaret Cameron. Nell Home is the girl with crutches. Nell was born on October 8th 1880. The wee girl in front of Mrs More could be her eldest daughter Sophia who was born on November 10th 1888. If so, this would date the photo to about 1891 or 92. Hugh Home, of Home's Close, is the man on the extreme right.

This is Margaret Owens and her husband James Cameron and daughter Ina. Margaret is the younger sister of my great-granny More.

This is Jenny Paterson's Auntie Maggie (Margaret Fraser) and her husband, Daniel MacKeddie, a mason, who died at Rosemarkie on February 8th 1912, aged 72. His wife Margaret died at Rosemarkie on July 26th 1930 aged 84.

Rosemarkie Youth 1920s Style – Back row: Sandy Hossack, Jimmy Miller. (The two men in uniform are marines stationed at The Poorhouse. It's called the Workhouse on the back of the photo) Alistair Ross, Donald Jack, Tom Owens, Bobby Owens; front: Maggie Bissett, Alistair Watson, Hattie Sinclair, Donnie Bissett, Jeannie Bissett, Alick Smith (this name on the back of the photo is a bit blurred), Kate Bissett, Alistair Fraser, William Home, Jock Owens.

Back, from left: Jock Ross (brother of Eck Ross), unknown, Tom Owens, Tom More, Robert More, George Fraser. Middle: Ken Jack (father of Jenny Paterson), Alistair Fraser ("the Banker"), Willie Hossack, uncle to Alistair and Billy Hossack who was home from America at the time this photo was taken. It is thought the man on the right with the whiskers is Hugh Munro. Seated, front: Jock Owens, unknown, Donnie Bisset.

According to Alistair Fraser in his booklet "Random Notes on Old Rosemarkie", a man called Davidson, was resident in Lilac Cottage in 1760 and in business there as a glover. This was considered a high class occupation in those days. I searched the burial records for Rosemarkie Churchyard and found a slab which reads: "This is the burial place of Donald Davidson, sometime dyster in Rosemarkie who died the (date missing), and here lys the body of Jean Fraser, his spouse, who died the 16th of Aprile 1786, aged 62 years."

Jeannie and Sandy Hossack and Mrs Leitham (Min Ross) at the door of Lilac Cottage.

From left: Sandy Hossack, Ephie Sinclair, Willie Hossack (brother of Sandy, resident in America), Dave Sinclair (father of Ephie).

Young and old at the beach c1922 – Back row: second left, Jock MacKeddie; third left, Achle Urquhart. Middle: second left, Willie Miller then Hugh MacLeman, Jimmy MacKeddie, Charlie Robb (Plough Inn). Front: first left, Jim Sinclair; sixth left, Rod Anderson; extreme right, Jack Junor.

At the tennis courts, early 1950s – Back, from left: Pheme Elder, George Elder, Janet Barnes, Fred MacLennan, George Elder snr; front: Barbara Elder, Alison Crawford, Doreen Elder, unknown, unknown, Fiona Crawford.

The tennis court was a good place to meet members of the opposite sex and romance was alive and well in the 50s. Here we have some of the local lads chatting up the Stornoway girls who came to Rosemarkie every summer to work in the hotel. Some of them married local lads. In this group are Charlie Grigor, Mark Grigor, Alistair Hossack, Willie Taylor, Ken Urquhart, and Katy-Mary who married Donnie Sutherland from Fortrose. The other two ladies are Ishbel Gunn, sister of Georgina Hossack, Rosemarkie and Dolina MacLeod from Stornoway.

Picnic on the beach – Front, from left: Alistair Hossack, Billy Hossack, unknown, Sandy Hossack; Ken Sinclair; back: unknown, Jeannie Hossack, Ephie Sinclair, Mrs Sinclair, unknown.

Rosemarkie Beach c1920s – Back, from left: John Smith (the Cabin), Mary Gallie, Minnie Fraser, Hugh MacKenzie, Sybil Campbell (Miller), Johnnie MacKenzie, Willie Malcolm.
Second row: Mrs Smith(?), Fred Fraser, Margaret MacKenzie (daughter of Johnnie), Ida MacKenzie (wife of Johnnie), Cath Miller.
Third row: Jess MacKenzie, Jean Miller (junior, from Glasgow), Hattie Sinclair, Jean Miller (Glasgow), Agnes Malcolm.
Front Row: Betty Malcolm, Alistair MacKenzie, Irene MacKenzie, Dot Miller (Glasgow).

The Social Scene

This group of players with a very politically-incorrect name – The Darkie Troup – was in existence for a number of years in the early 1900s. It was organised by Willie Young (known as Willie "Foof"), who is the man in the tile hat in the centre of the back row. On the extreme right of the back row is Donnie Bisset and next to him is Hugh Munro. In the middle row, 5th from left is Min Ross; next to her is George Fraser, then Janet Sinclair, an aunt of Pearl Sinclair. Tom More is the man in the white shirt and large bow and boater. Third from right in the middle row is Jeannie Bisset and 4th from the right is Edith Craig, sister of Mrs Masterton, the Manse. Next to Edith is Jimmy Stewart who lived in Bridge Street, son of Mrs MacDonald. He emigrated to South Africa. The man on the extreme left in the front row is an uncle of Alastair and Billy Hossack. He emigrated to America.

Willie Young is the man in the back row third from left in the black hat. Min Ross is third from left in the front row. Jeannie Bisset is third from the right in the front row. Donnie Bisset is extreme right of back row.

Dear John

I hope you are keeping quite well. Received your Photo with thanks hope you enjoyed the New Year. There is to be a concert of a darky troop and Father is to be ticket collector and Mother and all the tribe expects to get in for nothing I may tell you Mr Hossach Gallanhead was buried to day and Lizzie Kemp 3 weeks ago Willie Macandro has come home from south Africa Father will write you soon love from all from Jessie Miller

This postcard, stamped October 1906, is from Jessie Miller to her brother, Corporal John Miller, who was serving in the Armoured Service Corps in South Africa. Jessie's family lived in Kincurdie Cottage.

The Bisset family members were obviously budding performers as here we have Donnie (left), yet again, ready to take part in a production. Sister Maggie is also a member of the Darkie Troup. On the right is Willie Young who looks as if he's taking part in an outdoor performance.

This photo from the late fifties is probably of Rosemary Jones's birthday party and looks as if it is taking place in her house. Back, from left: Ray MacIntosh, Doreen Elder, Alison Crawford, Rosemary Jones, Bernice Smith, Trudy Binnie, Joan Cameron, John Cormack, May Whyte and Mrs Jones. Front: Catherine MacKenzie, Sandy Patience, Graham Jack, Flora Basham, Marion Smith, Maureen Young, Moira Miller, Lorna Corral. The wee blonde at the front is Janice Junor.

The WRI

Bus trip to Ballater – back, from left: Mag MacKenzie (Marita), Min Leitham (Ross, part view), Catherine Ross (mother of Helen and Robert Miller), Mrs Mary MacLennan, Vera Shaw (mother of Norma Sinclair), Lizzie Brooks, Jess Owens (Urquhart). Front: Jeannie Bissett, Jean-Ann More, Mary Denoon, Mrs Henderson.

Trip to Ullapool, 1953. Above, back, from left: unknown, Mrs Margaret Lackie, Rev Russell, Mrs Fraser, Mrs Junor, Mrs Cath More, Mrs Stronach. Front: unknown, Rhoda Anderson, Gina Gallie, Janet Grigor.

Right: The lady on the extreme right at the back is Bernice Smith (Junor) and next to her is the Rev Russell. The centre row consists of Mrs Henderson, Minnie Fraser (Smith) and Mary Denoon. Centre of the front row is Pheme Elder (Urquhart).

Possibly a WRI social sometime in the 50s. From left: Cathie Jones, Tot Hogg (Owens), Marie MacKenzie, Rita Cumming, Chris Miller, Mag MacKenzie (Marita, mother of Marie and Rita), Miss MacKenzie, Avoch. Note the modern, efficient, heating system in use in the Gordon Memorial Hall at that time!

WRI party, date unknown – back, from left: Joan MacLeman, Avoch; Isobel Currie; Betty Beattie (Geddes); Edith Grigor; Jessie Reid, Avoch; Gina Gallie; Jessie Junor; Marie MacKenzie; Marion Patience, Avoch. Front: Pheme Elder; Greta MacKenzie; Betty Young; Tot Young; Mrs Brooks, Fortrose; Joanie Mair (Barnes); Mrs MacKay (Royal Hotel, Fortrose).

Youth Club

Rosemarkie Youth Club was formed in the early 1950s by Mrs Margaret Crawford who lived in Tigh na Mara and later in the Old School, Rosemarkie. The club met once a week and members played badminton, table tennis and darts or listened to records and chatted over a cup of tea. Youth club members visited other youth clubs in Inverness and Beauly for social evenings, and regular dances were held, with live bands. A party was arranged at Christmas and every year the pensioners were also treated to a Christmas Party. From left: Roddy Shaw; Fiona Crawford; Roddy Shaw's girlfriend; Janet Barnes, Mary Grigor (behind Janet); Elspeth More; Freda Bassindale, Sheila MacKenzie. Front: Billy Hossack, Hugh MacKenzie;

David Smith throwing the darts. From left: Billy Hossack, Jonathan Owens, Hugh MacKenzie, John Redigan, Finlay MacLean, Bill MacLean and Tom MacLean.

Sheila MacKenzie (left) playing table tennis watched by Mary Grigor, Janet Barnes, Ann Anderson, Elspeth More, Freda Bassindale, Tom MacLean, George Elder and Billy Hossack. At the back are John Redigan, Jonathan Owens, Alistair Hossack and Bill MacLean.

In 1958 Rosemarkie Youth Club was invited to a Garden Party at Lauriston Castle attended by the Queen and Duke of Edinburgh. This happy group is pictured in Edinburgh's Princes Street Gardens. From left: Ena MacLean, Bill MacLean, Pearl More, Finlay MacLean, Dorothy Watt.

The Youth Club float taking part in the Coronation Parade in 1953. From left: Hugh MacKenzie, Norma Shaw, Charlie Grigor (partial view), Ken Urquhart, Helen Ross, Alistair Hossack, Isobel Millar. In front, in balaclava, Douglas Miller.

Isobel Miller, Elizabeth Anderson, Barbara Elder, Pearl More, Janet Barnes and George Elder enjoy the annual Christmas Party c1956. The efficient, modern heating system is still in use!

This photo was taken at an Easter Queen Beauty Contest dance held in the Gordon Memorial Hall, Rosemarkie on April 8th 1954. From left: Isobel Jack (Avoch), Winnie Barnes, Artie Barnes, Betty Barnes (Easter Queen), Helen Miller (runner-up), Joanie Barnes, Helen Ross (Muir of Ord).

Every year the Youth Club entertained the "Old Folks" with a party in the Gordon Memorial Hall. At this 1955 party, Janet Barnes (left) and Pat MacKeddie (right) are serving cakes to Jeannie Bissett, Mary Denoon, Ina Bissett, Lizzie Bissett, Ivy Gordon, Mary MacGillivray, Miss Fraser (Allanbank) Mrs Lumsden and the Rev Russell.

Wartime

The Boer War

These are three Boer War veterans. This photo is believed to have been taken in South Africa, c1900 and the men are in the uniform of the Lovat Scouts.

I was told that the middle man was Daniel MacIver, son of Sandy and Mary MacIver of Greenside, but in the census of 1891, Sandy and Mary have seven children, none of whom is called Daniel. Daniel, however, might be the son of Sandy MacIver and Jane Home, making him a brother of Sandy MacIver, Greenside. The identity of the other two men is unknown.

The Scottish Highland Regiment of the Lovat Scouts was formed in January 1900 by the 14th Lord Lovat. On a website listing the Lovat Scouts who served in the Boer War, I found the name, Donald MacIver, 8816, Private, Lovat Scouts.

World War I

Left: Daniel Fraser in the uniform of the Seaforth Highlanders.

Right: An unknown soldier.

Robert More was Rosemarkie's very own War Hero. Born in 1897, Robert took the ferry across the firth from Chanonry Point to Fort George where he tried to join the Seaforth Highlanders. When they discovered his age, he was sent back.

Undaunted, Robert joined the Black Watch Territorials, aged 14, while he was working as a forester near Perth. He was successful in getting transferred to the Seaforth Highlanders, Territorials at Fort George and was promoted to the rank of Sergeant by the time he was 16.

When war broke out in 1914, Robert was 17 and working in Caithness. He was enlisted into the regular army and sent to the Western Front where he served throughout the war. He took part in the 1914 Christmas Truce, when the celebrations lasted all day and the opposing armies exchanged souvenirs such as buttons and envelopes with stamps. He fought at Neuve Chapelle and took part in both battles of the Somme.

Robert was wounded three times. He was awarded the Distinguished Conduct Medal for bravery in the field and the Military Medal (and Bar a year later.) He was also awarded the Croix de Guerre.

The Ross-shire Journal reported on Friday September 14th 1917, that Robert, while home on leave, was honoured by the residents of Rosemarkie with a reception followed by a social evening in the Gordon Memorial Hall. He was presented with a gold watch and chain.

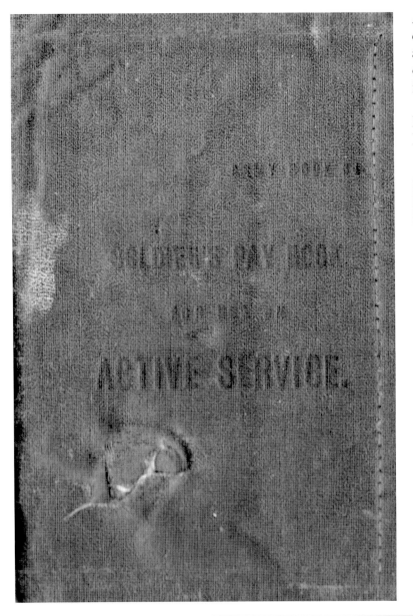

At Neuve Chapelle, a bullet struck Robert in the chest. He didn't realise at first that he'd been hit, but later he discovered a bullet still embedded in his New Testament and paybook containing a photo of the King and Queen, which he carried in his breast pocket.

Left: Robert More's army paybook complete with bullet hole.
Below: The damaged photo

Ken Jack and Robert More

Back, from left: 3rd left James Fraser (Towny, brother of George and Daniel Fraser); 4th left Jimmy Stewart, Bridge Street; 5th left Donnie Bissett. Front: 3rd left George Hossack; extreme right is Jock MacIver, son of Sandy and Mary, Greenside.

This photo was probably taken during World War I and shows Rosemarkie youth sitting on the old canon which used to sit in the churchyard. I've no idea where it came from, but apparently it was removed during World War II when all the iron railings were removed from public buildings to be used in the manufacture of aeroplanes and tanks. From left: Ken Jack, father of Jenny Paterson; Liz Jack, sister of Ken; George Fraser; Tom More. The identities of the man in the dark suit and the man in the tartan trews, are not known. The youth sitting at the front is Beelack MacAndrew.

World War II

In 1939 the army arrived in force in Rosemarkie. The Marine Hotel was requisitioned and became the Army HQ. The MacKenzie family were given 48 hours to quit the Marita Boarding House which became the Officers' Mess. Most of the large villas in Marine Terrace housed troops. Redholm, now known as Kinkell, was accidentally set on fire by the troops living there, while Craigview in Bridge Street was also accidentally burnt down by the Polish soldiers. Polish soldiers were also billeted in Eck Ross's garage in Bridge Street, and to help ease their homesickness, they painted the Polish flag on one of the garage walls. I believe it is still there. The RAF built and operated an airfield at Blackstand and Canadian foresters from Newfoundland were engaged in saw-milling along at Learnie. A Norwegian unit operated on the Golf Course.

In 1942 King Haakon of Norway came to Rosemarkie to review the Norwegian troops and to present them with campaign medals. The inspection took place in the field that is now Gollanhead. After the presentation, the King walked down the High Street and had lunch in the Marita. This photo, taken on the golf course, shows the King on the extreme left of the picture. Crown Prince Olav is second right.

Chanonry Point played a crucial role in the D-Day landings which began on June 6th 1944, when the allies launched an all-out attack on the Germans in Europe. The Black Isle roads from Kessock to Rosemarkie were choked with hundreds of armoured tanks which trundled down the Ness Road towards the golf course where they embarked on large amphibian craft to be transported along the coast to Moray. These were training exercises for D-Day.

The amphibian craft came into the sloping beach at the north end of the golf course between the clubhouse and the

George Gallie, on the left, was born on September 25th 1918. Just prior to the outbreak of the war, George joined the Seaforth Highlanders. When war broke out in 1939 he was stationed at Fort George.

Willie Miller, on the right, also joined the Seaforth Highlanders and in early 1940 they were part of the force that fought a rearguard action and made an important contribution to the evacuation of troops from Dunkirk.

George was reported missing in action on June 12th 1940 while fighting at St Valery en Caux and it wasn't until late 1940 that his family received a letter from him saying that he was a POW in Stalag 8B. He remained there until May 21st 1945.

lighthouse and were secured to the many concrete blocks built there for the purpose. Some of the concrete blocks can still be seen embedded in the sand dunes. The exercises began at nightfall and I remember as a child being taken out to the front door of our house at the Ness to hear the tanks rumbling past.

It wasn't all gloom and doom in Rosemarkie during World War II. The airfield at Blackstand was the hub of the forces' social life and every weekend buses ferried scores of young ladies to concerts and dances there. The troops also held Christmas parties for local children and took part in the social life of the village. The canteen in the Gordon Memorial Hall and Ross's Café in the High Street were both popular with the troops.

Tommy Stott (above) was a cousin of my father and was brought up, together with his sister Margaret, by Granny More in 5 Bridge Street. After the war he left Rosemarkie in search of work and ended up in Edinburgh where I met him in the 1960s. He had two brothers and two sisters living in Kenmore but was not in touch with them. He occasionally visited his uncle Robert More in Rosemarkie. Very little was known about his life in Edinburgh, but I discovered that he was reunited with his family in Kenmore before he died. His ashes were scattered in Rosemarkie Churchyard.

Donald Gallie in North Africa

It wasn't just the men who went to war in 1939. Marie MacKenzie was a few days short of her 18th birthday when she went to Cameron Barracks, Inverness to join the ATS.

Coming from a small village has its advantages sometimes. During the war, Marie was boarding a train in London, heading for Inverness. The train was crowded and there were no seats left in second class. She met fellow Rosemarkie resident, Mr Tarrell, who, as an officer in charge of the Observer Corps, was entitled to travel first class and he invited her into his compartment where she travelled in relative comfort to Inverness. Strictly against army rules of course.

Marie with friend Iris.

In 1939 a unit of the Royal Observer Corps was formed. A large concrete observer post was built on the golf course across the road from the ninth tee. Those who were too old to be called up and those who were exempt from service due to ill health joined the Observer Corps. Under the management of Mr Tarrel from Rosemarkie, the unit remained in operation until the end of the war. Back, from left: Charlie MacKenzie, Mr Tarrel, Danny Chisholm George Brooks, Hugh Penney. Front: Tom More, Jock MacKeddie, Davy Steven, George MacFarlane.